MW00947504

THE GREAT BOOK OF ANIMAL KNOWLEDGE

ZEBRAS

Striped Wild Horses of Africa

All Rights Reserved. All written content in this book may NOT be reproduced in any form or by any means, including scanning, photocopying, or otherwise without prior written permission of the copyright holder. Copyright © 2014

Some Rights Reserved. All photographs contained in this book are under the Creative Commons license and can be copied and redistributed in any medium or format for any purpose, even commercially. However, you must give appropriate credit, provide a link to the license, and indicate if changes were made.

Introduction

Photo by Barbara Eckstein (flickr.com/beckstei), as licensed under CC BY 2.0 Generic

The zebra is one of the most recognizable animals because of their black and white stripes. There are three species of zebras, namely the plain zebras, mountain zebras, and Grevy's zebras. The main differences between these three are their habitats and stripes. The zebra was named after the Latin word equiferus meaning "wild horse."

What Zebras Look Like

Photo by Filip Lachowski (flickr.com/malczyk), as licensed under CC BY-SA 2.0 Generic

Zebras look like horses, but have black and white stripes. Unlike the horse, the zebra's mane is short and straight. The zebra's tail has a clutter of long hair at the bottom.

Size and Weight

Photo by snarglebart (flickr.com/77272877@N00), as licensed under CC BY-SA 2.0 Generic

Zebras are 4 feet from their shoulder downwards, and 6 to 8 feet long including a 1 foot tail. They weigh about 770 pounds. Male zebras are slightly bigger than female zebras.

Senses

Photo by paulshaffner (flickr.com/paulshaffner), as licensed under CC BY 2.0 Generic

Zebras have very good senses. They need a good sense of seeing and hearing to be aware of approaching enemies. They also have excellent tastes buds, allowing them to notice slight changes in their food quality.

Stripes

Photo by Martin Pettitt (flickr.com/mdpettitt), as licensed under CC BY 2.0 Generic

Zebras are most known for their black and white stripes. Each individual zebra has its own unique stripe pattern. Their stripes are used for controlling the heat, and for making zebras able to recognize each other by their different stripe patterns. Also, when zebras are together, their stripes merge into a big mass and make it hard for their predators to single out one zebra.

Sleeping

Photo by Bernard DUPONT (flickr.com/berniedup), as licensed under CC BY-SA 2.0 Generic

Zebras sleep standing up! They stand up while sleeping so that it will be easier to escape if a predator attacks. Zebras only sleep when they're in large groups, though, so that they can be warned of danger by the other members that are not sleeping.

Where Zebras Live

Photo by Filip Lachowski (flickr.com/malczyk), as licensed under CC BY-SA 2.0 Generic

Zebras are found in Africa. The three zebra species live in different habitats. Grevy's zebras live in sub-desert places. The plain zebras have many habitats, ranging from the savanna, to open woodlands, to grasslands. The mountain zebras, as you can tell, live in the mountains or hilly places.

What Zebras Eat

Photo by Marieke IJsendoorn-Kuijpers (flickr.com/mape_s), as licensed under CC BY 2.0 Generic

Zebras are herbivores, meaning they eat only plants. Zebras feed on many different plants, like shrubs, herbs, twigs, leaves, fruits, crops, roots, bark; but they prefer to eat green grass.

Harems

Photo by Filip Lachowski (flickr.com/malczyk), as licensed under CC BY-SA 2.0 Generic

Zebras are very social animals and live in groups called harems. Plain and mountain zebras live in harems that are made up of one stallion - male, and up to six mares - female, and their young; while Grevy's zebras come together as groups for short periods of time only. Sometimes, different harems temporarily come together to form a group, called a herd, of more than 30 members.

Grooming

Photo by René Mayorga (flickr.com/elchurro), as licensed under CC BY-SA 2.0 Generic

Grooming in harems is an important activity to create strong bonds within the family. Zebras will use their teeth and lips to nibble along the neck, shoulders, and back of the zebra they're grooming. Besides creating strong bonds, grooming can also ease aggression within a zebra.

Communication

Photo by Artonk (flickr.com/91777723@N02), as licensed under CC BY 2.0 Generic

Zebras communicate with each other through sound and body language. For sounds, they communicate by barking, braying, or snorting. The importance of their communication is based on how pitched and intense their sound is. The position of their ears, how wide their eyes are opened, and whether their mouth is opened, closed, or with teeth bared, are all part of the body language communication.

Migration

Photo by Max Handelsman (flickr.com/maxh42), as licensed under CC BY-SA 2.0 Generic

Every year, plain and mountain zebras migrate during the dry season in search for water and greener pastures. Harems join together in migrating seasons, making a super large migrating zebra group. Zebras don't migrate by themselves; they are usually seen traveling with other animals, like the wildebeest.

Breeding

Photo by NH53 (flickr.com/ nh53), as licensed under CC BY 2.0 Generic

Breeding seasons for the zebra is January to March. A female zebra will only become pregnant if she is mated at her most fertile period in her heat. Females can start mating at 1 year old, but will only become pregnant when they reach the age of 2. A female will be pregnant for a year.

Baby Zebras

Photo by Bob Steiner (flickr.com/ bobsteiner), as licensed under CC BY-SA 2.0 Generic

Baby zebras are called foals. A mother zebra gives birth to just one foal at a time. Foals are born with their stripes; however, their stripes appear to be colored brown and white. The mother hides her newborn foal from the other members for a short time, so that the foal will learn to identify her by her sight, smell and sound. A foal is able to stand up by itself in 15 minutes, and in 1 hour it can already walk beside its mother.

Life of a Zebra

Photo by Chadica (flickr.com/chadica), as licensed under CC BY 2.0 Generic

A foal is fully trained between 7 to 11 months, but they continue to drink their mother's milk until 1 year old. They are independent when they reach 1 year old and a male foal will leave his family and make his own harem, but if he doesn't want to move yet he can stay with his harem for 4 more years. However, foals don't usually survive the first year because they are the main aim for predators. If they do survive, they can live for up to 9 years.

Predators

Photo by alistair.pott (flickr.com/ alistairpott), as licensed under CC BY-SA 2.0 Generic

Zebras have a lot of predators, including lions, hyenas, wolves, leopards, cheetahs, and even crocodiles. These predators usually catch the foals and ill zebras; however, if the predators come in a pack they can kill even a healthy, adult zebra.

A Zebras Defense

Photo by devra (flickr.com/ minicooper93402), as licensed under CC BY 2.0 Generic

Zebras are very fast runners, allowing them to outrun their predators. If they do get caught, they have strong back legs so they can kick their predators in the face; they can also use their teeth for biting. And when a group of zebras are being chased, the males will surround the females and foals to protect them while running. Zebras also run in a zigzag way so that it will be harder for the predators to catch them.

Threats

Photo by Barbara Eckstein (flickr.com/ beckstei), as licensed under CC BY 2.0 Generic

Only Grevy's zebras are endangered, meaning there are only a few of them left. But all zebra species are facing threats; not only because of them being prey to some animals, but also because of poachers, hunters that kill them for their fur, lack of water, and habitat loss. Habitat lose happens when people claim an area to make farms.

Plain Zebras

Photo by Derek Keats (flickr.com/ dkeats), as licensed under CC BY 2.0 Generic

The plain zebra is the most common kind of zebra but also the smallest kind. They have wide stripes that run horizontally towards the back and vertically towards the front.

Mountain Zebras

Photo by John5199 (flickr.com/ jonnyb558), as licensed under CC BY 2.0 Generic

The mountain zebras have thin, vertical stripes that are close together in their neck and chest. The stripes become wide and horizontal in their back and feet. The spaces between the stripes also grow bigger in their back and feet.

Grevy's Zebras

Photo by adam w (flickr.com/ asw909), as licensed under CC BY 2.0 Generic

Grevy's zebras are the most unique zebras. Their stripes are very close to each other and have different patterns. Their stripes also extend all the way down to their hooves. And they have a wide, black stripe along their back and no stripes on their stomachs. The Grevy's zebras also have white tipped ears.

Get the next book in this series!

WARTHOGS: Tusked Hogs of Africa

Log on to Facebook.com/GazelleCB for more info

Tip: Use the key-phrase "The Great Book of Animal Knowledge" when searching for books in this series.

For more information about our books, discounts and updates, please Like us on FaceBook!

Facebook.com/GazelleCB

37717190R00017

Made in the USA
Middletown, DE
05 December 2016